Welcome to xtb Issue Two

Miracles and Dreams

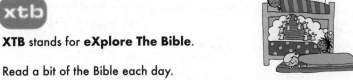

XTB stands for **eXplore The Bible**.

Read a bit of the Bible each day.
Meet Jacob the Schemer and Joseph the Dreamer in the book of **Genesis**.
Zoom in on **Matthew** and **Acts** to find out who Jesus is and why He came.

Are you ready to explore the Bible? Fill in the bookmark...
...then turn over the page to start exploring with XTB!

Table Talk FOR FAMILIES

Look out for **Table Talk** — a book to help children and
adults explore the Bible together. It can be used by:

- Families
- One adult with one child
- Children's leaders with their groups
- Any other way you want to try

Table Talk uses the same Bible passages as XTB so that they can be used together
if wanted. You can buy Table Talk from your local Good Book Company website:
UK: www.thegoodbook.co.uk • North America: www.thegoodbook.com
Australia: www.thegoodbook.com.au • New Zealand: www.thegoodbook.co.nz

This book belongs to

....

Sometimes I'm called

.... (nickname)

My birthday is

....

My age is

....

My favourite ice-cream flavour is

....

OLD TESTAMENT	NEW TESTAMENT
Genesis	**Matthew**
Exodus	Mark
Leviticus	Luke
Numbers	John
Deuteronomy	**Acts**
Joshua	Romans
Judges	1 Corinthians
Ruth	2 Corinthians
1 Samuel	Galatians
2 Samuel	Ephesians
1 Kings	Philippians
2 Kings	Colossians
1 Chronicles	1 Thessalonians
2 Chronicles	2 Thessalonians
Ezra	1 Timothy
Nehemiah	2 Timothy
Esther	Titus
Job	Philemon
Psalms	Hebrews
Proverbs	James
Ecclesiastes	1 Peter
Song of Solomon	2 Peter
Isaiah	1 John
Jeremiah	2 John
Lamentations	3 John
Ezekiel	Jude
Daniel	Revelation
Hosea	
Joel	
Amos	
Obadiah	
Jonah	
Micah	
Nahum	
Habakkuk	
Zephaniah	
Haggai	
Zechariah	
Malachi	

How to find your way around the Bible

Look out for the **READ** sign.
It tells you what Bible bit to read.

So, if the notes say... READ Acts 8v4-8
...this means chapter 8 and verses 4 to 8
...and this is how you find it.

READ
Acts 8v4-8

Use the **Contents** page in your Bible to find
where Acts begins

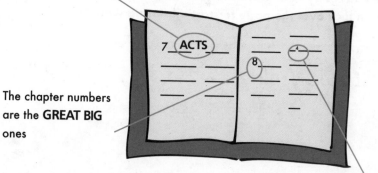

The chapter numbers
are the **GREAT BIG**
ones

7 ACTS

The verse numbers are the
tiny ones!

Oops! Keep getting lost?
Cut out this bookmark and use it to keep your place.

How to use xtb

1 Find a time and place when you can read the Bible each day.

2  Get your Bible, a pencil and your XTB notes.

3  Ask God to help you to understand what you read.

4  Read today's XTB page and Bible bit.

5  Pray about what you have read and learned.

6  If you can, talk to an adult or a friend about what you've learned.

CRACK THE CODES

This copy of XTB is packed full of codes to crack.

We'll use them to explore three Bible books—Genesis, Matthew and Acts. You can use them to write secret messages to your friends too!

You'll find all the codes inside the back cover.

Are you ready to try your hand as a Code Cracker? Then hurry on to Day 1.

DAY 1   MEET THE ACTion MEN

The key to the book of Acts is found at the very beginning. In Acts 1v8, Jesus told His followers:

> "But when the Holy Spirit comes upon you, you will be filled with power, and you will be witnesses for me in **Jerusalem**, in all **Judea** and **Samaria**, and to the **ends of the earth**." *Acts 1v8*

The rest of Acts is the story of 1v8 coming true as Jesus' followers tell other people all about Him
—first in **Jerusalem**
—then in **Judea** and **Samaria**
—and then further and further and further...

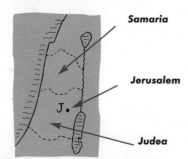

Samaria

Jerusalem

Judea

In chapters 8 to 10 of ACTS we'll meet three ACTion men. Their main ACT was to tell people all about Jesus.

They are **Philip**,   **Paul**   and **Peter**.

The Story of ACTS so far...

- Jesus' followers were called **Christians**—because they believed in Jesus <u>Christ</u>.

- They had the job of being **Chatterboxes**—telling other people about Jesus. But this got them into B–I–G trouble!

- The powerful Jewish leaders <u>hated</u> what the Christians were saying about Jesus. They tried all kinds of ways to make them stop—they had Christians whipped, put in prison or even killed!

- It was **too dangerous** to stay in Jerusalem, so many Christians left. And everywhere they went—they told more people about Jesus!

Find out more on the next page

SCATTERED!

Acts
8v4-8

Use the Arrow Code to find out **who** today's story is about, and **where** he is. (*The Arrow Code is on the back cover.*)

Who?

_ _ _ _ _ _

Where?

_ _ _ _ _ _ _

READ
Acts 8v4-8

Jesus' followers were scattered throughout **Judea** and **Samaria**.
(*Find them on the map opposite.*)
Everywhere they went, they carried on being chatterboxes—telling people about Jesus.

Philip went to a city in Samaria, where he told the people all about Jesus. What was the result?

_ _ _ _ _ _   _ _ _ _ _

THINK SPOT

Jesus had told His followers that they would be "*witnesses for Him in Jerusalem, in all Judea and Samaria...*" (Acts 1v8).
His enemies wanted to <u>stop</u> the news about Jesus from spreading. But instead, they made it spread even further!! God's plans can <u>never</u> be stopped!!!

THINK + PRAY

Jesus promised that the message about Him would also spread to "the ends of the earth." His promise came true. It has spread to you and me as well! Who tells <u>you</u> about Jesus?

_____

Ask God to help them.

All through Acts we see how the Holy Spirit helped Christians to tell others about Jesus. But someone in today's story got the wrong end of the stick! His name was Simon...

SIMON
Lived in Samaria. He had made a name for himself doing **magic**. Crowds of people followed him.

PHILIP
When Philip came to Samaria, the Holy Spirit helped him to tell people about **Jesus**. Many people believed—including Simon.

PETER and JOHN
Came to visit Samaria when they heard that the people believed in Jesus. They prayed that the people would be given the Holy Spirit to help them. They were!

The Holy Spirit would help the people to serve God and to tell others about Jesus. But Simon misunderstood...

READ
Acts 8v18-25

Simon wanted to be able to give people the Holy Spirit too. What did he offer to Peter and John?

Use the
Pig Pen Code →

▫ ▪ ▫ ▢ ⌂
— — — — —

But Peter knew what Simon's problem was...

Your _ _ _ _ _ is not right

before God. (v21)

Simon had been very wrong to think that he could <u>buy</u> anything from God. He asked Peter + John to pray for him. Peter told Simon to **repent**. He had to turn away from his wrong ways.

Did you know?

The Holy Spirit is a **free gift** to <u>everyone</u> who follows Jesus. The Spirit helps us to live for God, and to tell other people about Jesus too.

If you are following Jesus, then <u>you</u> have the Holy Spirit to help you too.

THINK + PRAY

Thank God for giving you His Spirit, and ask Him to help you to live for Him.

CHARIOT CHATTERBOX

1 Do you understand the angel's message to Philip?
Use Morse code (inside the back cover)

- - • / - - -   • • • / - - - / • • - / - / • • • •

— — — — — — — — —

The angel told Philip to leave Samaria and go south.
There was someone he needed to meet...

2

What was this
Ethiopian man
reading?

• • / • • • • / • - / • • - / • - / • • • •

— — — — — — —

The book of Isaiah is in the Old Testament part of the Bible.
Isaiah wrote about **Jesus**—but his book is quite hard to
understand. The Ethiopian didn't know **who** he was reading
about. He needed help...

3 **READ**
Acts 8v29-35

 Philip told the Ethiopian
all about **Jesus**.

It wasn't <u>luck</u> that Philip met this Ethiopian. **God** planned it.
Why do you think God wanted them to meet?

4 The Ethiopian needed someone to explain the
Bible to him—so God provided Philip.

THINK + PRAY Do <u>you</u> have someone who helps
you to understand the Bible?

YES
Thank God for
them, and ask Him
to help them.

NO
Ask God to provide
someone who can
help you.

STOP THAT CHARIOT!

Philip and the Ethiopian were in a chariot. When they came to some water, the Ethiopian commanded the chariot to stop. Why do you think they stopped?

?
a) To wash the chariot
b) To get a drink
c) To have a swim
d) Something else

Read the next part of Acts to find out...

READ
Acts 8v36-40

What did Philip do? (v38)

He **b**_____
the Ethiopian.

Did you know?

People were baptised by being dunked under the water. It showed that they were trusting Jesus to wash away their sins, and that they would live for Him from now on.

What happened next? (v39-40)

(Cross out the wrong answers.)

• Philip **disappeared / stayed**.
• The Ethiopian was **sad / full of joy**.
• Philip **carried on / stopped** being a chatterbox about Jesus.

THINK + PRAY

God wants the **whole world** to know about Jesus. Philip carried on telling others about Jesus. And when the Ethiopian went home, he probably told people in Africa about Jesus too.

Today the good news about Jesus has spread to every country in the world— just as Jesus said it would in Acts 1v8. Thank God that the news about Jesus has reached **you** too.

SAUL'S SHOCK

All through Acts we see that the message about Jesus can't be stopped. In today's story, Saul <u>tries</u> to stop it—but instead **God** stops Saul!

SAUL STORY
- Saul was a **Pharisee**—a Jewish religious leader.
- Saul **didn't believe** that Jesus was the Son of God.
- Saul **hated** Christians. He had them thrown into prison!

The news about Jesus was spreading far and wide. One place it had reached was the city of **Damascus**, in Syria. Saul decided to go there (about a week's walk) to hunt out any followers of Jesus. He wanted to have them dragged back to Jerusalem...

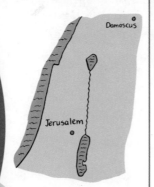

Damascus

Jerusalem

READ
Acts 9v3-9

Fill in the missing words from verse 5.

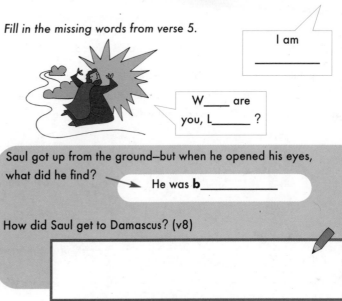

I am
_____

W____ are you, L_____ ?

Saul got up from the ground—but when he opened his eyes, what did he find?

He was **b**_____

How did Saul get to Damascus? (v8)

THINK + PRAY

Saul thought he could <u>stop</u> the message about Jesus—but He was wrong! **God** was always in control. Thank God that **nothing** and **no one** can stop His plans.

DAY 6 BLINDING STUFF!

Saul waited in Damascus for three days, eating and drinking nothing. He was still blind.

Meanwhile, God spoke to another follower of Jesus who was in Damascus. God had a special job for this man to do. Solve the puzzle to find out **who** he was and **where** he had to go.

Rocky Road

Long Lane

Clip-Clop Close

Straight Street

Wilderness Way

⅃ ⊔ ⅃ ⊔ ⅃ ⌐ ⅃ ∨
‾ ‾ ‾ ‾ ‾ ‾ ‾

Use the **Pig Pen Code** inside the back cover

Find out more by reading the next part of Acts...

READ
Acts 9v10-19

Ananias had heard about the terrible things Saul had been doing. How do you think he felt when God told him to go and see Saul? (*Circle your answers and add more of your own.*)

Surprised   Puzzled   Angry

Scared   Excited   Pleased

When Ananias placed his hands on Saul, what fell from Saul's eyes?

Once Saul could see again, he got up and was baptised. He was now a follower of Jesus too!

THINK + PRAY

It must have been hard for Ananias to go and help Saul. But he <u>obeyed</u> God. Ask God to help you to be like Ananias—and to obey God even when it's hard.

DAY 7 — BASKET CASE

Flick back to yesterday's reading to see what God said that Saul would do.

READ
Acts 9v15

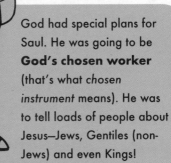

God had special plans for Saul. He was going to be **God's chosen worker** (that's what *chosen instrument* means). He was to tell loads of people about Jesus—Jews, Gentiles (non-Jews) and even Kings!

Saul started right away...

READ
Acts 9v19-22

The people who heard Saul were amazed! They knew he had come to Damascus to arrest Jesus' followers. But now Saul was being a chatterbox for Jesus instead!

Cross out every **X**, **Y** & **Z** to see what Saul was teaching.

> *Did You Know?*
>
> **Christ** (Greek) and **Messiah** (Hebrew) both mean "God's chosen King".

Saul was a follower of Jesus now. The Jewish leaders weren't happy. One of their best men had changed sides! They wanted to get rid of him...

READ
Acts 9v23-25

How did Saul escape?

Draw or write your answer here.

THINK + PRAY

God kept Saul safe so that he could go and tell other people about Jesus. Who can <u>you</u> tell about Jesus?

_____

Ask God to help you.

DAY 8 ALL CHANGE

Saul had escaped from Damascus in a basket! He returned to Jerusalem, where he wanted to meet with the other followers of Jesus. But there was a problem...

Last time Saul was in Jerusalem he had been dragging Jesus' followers from their homes and throwing them into **prison**! How do you think they'd feel about Saul coming to join them?

No Way!

It must be a trap.

Great!

Maybe he really has changed...

READ
Acts 9v26-30

The believers were very scared of Saul. But who took Saul to meet their leaders, the apostles? (v27)

Use the Arrow Code

— — — — — — — — —

Did You know?

Barnabas means "Son of Encouragement" (Acts 4v36)

Barnabas told the apostles how much Saul had **changed**. The other believers now welcomed Saul. He stayed with them in Jerusalem, and carried on being a chatterbox about Jesus.

But talking about Jesus got Saul into danger—**again!**—and he had to leave Jerusalem. He escaped to the city of Tarsus, his home town.

THINK SPOT

Wow! What a H-U-G-E **change** in Saul! He can't stop talking about Jesus—even when that puts him into danger.

When someone becomes a follower of Jesus they always **change**. God gives them His Holy Spirit to help them to live for Him, and to help them become more like Jesus.

THINK + PRAY

If you are following Jesus, **you** should expect to change too. Have you noticed any changes? (Maybe you love reading the Bible now? Or find that you think of others before yourself? Or you don't tell lie any more? If you're not sure, ask Christian friend what they think.) Ask God to **keep changing you**, so that you become more and more like Jesus.

DAY 9 GROWING ON

Enlarge this picture by copying one square at a time.

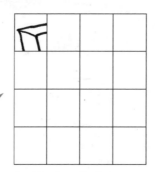

What grows in today's reading? (*Use the Number Code.*)

7 19 22   24 19 6 9 24 19

__ __ __   __ __ __ __ __ __

READ
Acts 9v31

Verse 31 says that the church was **growing**.
What do you think that means?

a) That the church building was made bigger.

b) That more churches were built.

c) That more people became followers of Jesus.

Did you know?

When the Bible talks about the <u>church</u> it never means a **building**. It always means **people**.

These people didn't have special buildings to meet in. Often they met in their homes. And more and more of them were meeting together as Christians—followers of Jesus. The church was <u>growing</u>.

Who encouraged the Christians and helped them to serve God?

The **H**_____ **S**_____

THINK + PRAY

The Holy Spirit helps Christians to serve God and to tell others about Jesus. What kind of help do you need most at the moment?

- Help to tell your friends about Jesus
- Help to put God first in your life
- Help to know God better
- Help with all of these!

Ask God to help you.

MAKE YOUR BED!

How do you feel when you're told to make your bed?

> Ohh... Do I have to?

> Yippee—I love making beds!

> Can I do it later?

The man in today's story was told to make his bed—and it was **great news!**

READ
Acts 9v32-35

How long had Aeneas been stuck in bed? (v33)

[   ] **years**

But now Peter had some great news for Aeneas...

Fill in the gaps

J_____ C_____ heals you. G_____ U____ and make your bed. (v34)

Wow! What an amazing miracle! Aeneas was healed at once! But there's an even <u>more</u> amazing miracle in this story. Did you spot it?

> It's in verse 35

Did you know?

When someone turns to God it's a **miracle**. It is our nature to turn our <u>backs</u> on God and ignore Him. It's only possible for us to believe in Jesus and turn <u>to</u> God because God Himself makes it possible. It's a **miracle!**

Read v35 *and cross out the wrong words.*

One person / ten people / everyone in Sharon and London / Lydda / Lisbon got excited / went fishing / turned to God

Are <u>you</u> like those people in Lydda and Sharon? Have you turned to God?

If you have, thank God for doing a **miracle** in your life.

THINK + PRAY

If you're not sure, keep reading the book of Acts. Peter has more important stuff to say about how <u>everyone</u> can turn to God.

DAY 11 D DAY

 Acts 9v36-43

Solve the puzzle using the Shape Code.

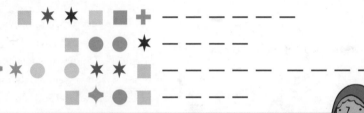

■ ★ ★ ■ ■ ✚ _ _ _ _ _ _
■ ● ● ★ _ _ _ _
■ ★ ✦ ★ ● ● ★ ★ ■ _ _ _ _ _ _ _ _
■ ✦ ● ■ _ _ _ _ _

Use these words to fill in the gaps.

D_____ was a Christian who lived in Joppa. Her name means

D_____ . She was always D_____ _____ and helping

the poor. But sadly, Dorcas became ill and D_____

The other Christians sent for Peter, and asked him to come at once.

READ
Acts 9v39-41

Dorcas (also called Tabitha) really was dead. But what did Peter say to her? (v40)

Wow! Another amazing miracle! Dorcas came back to life!

What do you think happened when people heard about Dorcas?

READ
v 42-43 to find out.

More and more people became Christians. Each one was another **miracle**!!

THINK + PRAY

Look back at v36.
Dorcas was "always doing good and helping the poor". Do you want to be like Dorcas? If you do, that's great! But it won't always be easy. Ask God to help you.

DOUBLE VISION

Peter and the other disciples are to be **chatterboxes** about Jesus. But up until now they have mainly been telling <u>Jewish</u> people about Jesus. They need to understand that the message about Jesus is for <u>everyone</u>.

Time to set the scene for a H—U—G—E meeting between **Peter** (a Jew) and a Roman Centurion called **Cornelius** (a non-Jew)...

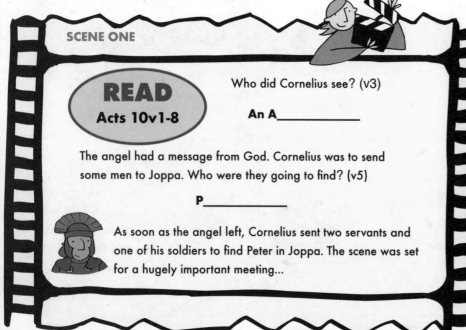

SCENE ONE

READ
Acts 10v1-8

Who did Cornelius see? (v3)

An A_____

The angel had a message from God. Cornelius was to send some men to Joppa. Who were they going to find? (v5)

P_____

As soon as the angel left, Cornelius sent two servants and one of his soldiers to find Peter in Joppa. The scene was set for a hugely important meeting...

Yesterday we saw how Dorcas was "always doing good". Today, Acts tells us that Cornelius "gave generously to those in need and prayed to God regularly". (v2)

THINK + PRAY

How do <u>you</u> match up to Cornelius?
- *Do you find ways to give to people who have less than you?*
- *Do you pray regularly?*

Talk to God about your answers and ask Him to help you.

PS Why is today's page called **Double Vision**? Because tomorrow, Peter will have a vision too...

DAY 13 PETER'S VISION

The action shifts from Cornelius to Peter. It's lunchtime the next day, and Peter is hungry. Suddenly he has a vision—and it's all about food! But Peter's not dreaming—it's a message from God...

SCENE TWO

READ
Acts 10v9-16

Peter saw a sheet coming down from heaven. What was in the sheet? (v12)

Draw or write your answer here.

Use these words to fill in the gaps.

Peter   eat   never   Lord   unclean

Get up, _____. Kill and _____.

Surely not, _____ ! I have _____ eaten anything impure or _____

Did you know?

Peter was a Jew, so he followed all the Old Testament rules about food. Food that Jews were allowed to eat was called CLEAN. Forbidden food was called UNCLEAN.

The sheet Peter saw had a mix of clean and unclean animals in it. That's why Peter was so shocked.

Peter had a very important lesson to learn...

Do not call anything impure that **G_____** has called clean. (v15)

PRAY

Peter was shocked, and found it hard to believe what God was saying. Ask God to help <u>you</u> when you find it hard to believe or understand what He is saying in the Bible.

Peter's dream <u>seemed</u> to be about food. But was it?? *Find out tomorrow in Scene Three...*

DAY 14 CLEANING UP

SCENE THREE

Peter was puzzled by his dream.

Then three men arrived.

Cornelius sent us.

The Holy Spirit told Peter to go with the men.

Don't hesitate to go with these men, for *I have sent them.*

So Peter went to meet Cornelius...

You know it's against our law for a Jew to visit a non-Jew.

But God has shown me that I should not call *anyone* unclean.

READ
Acts 10v27-33

- **Who** told Peter not to call anyone unclean? (v28) **G____**
- **Who** sent an angel to Cornelius? (v3) **G____**
- Now Cornelius had collected a crowd together. They knew Peter would have a message for them from **G____** (v33)

THINK SPOT

Peter's dream seemed to be about <u>food</u>—but God was really teaching Peter about <u>people</u>. Jews (like Peter) thought of non-Jews (like Cornelius) as **unclean.** But God showed Peter that this was wrong. The great news about Jesus is for **EVERYONE**.

PRAY **Thank God that the good news about Jesus is for everyone—including <u>you</u>.**

PETE'S NEAT SPEECH

Acts 10v34-41

Cornelius had called a crowd together to hear what Peter was going to say. Let's listen in...

SCENE FOUR

Use the **FLAG** code

God doesn't have

_ _ _ _ _ _ _ _ _ _ _

The good news about _ _ _ _ _
is for everyone!

Jesus was _ _ _ _ _ _
but God brought Him back to life.

I'm a _ _ _ _ _ _ _ _

Read part of Peter's speech for yourself...

READ
Acts 10v39-41

It must have been hard to believe that Jesus came back from the dead—but Peter was a **witness** (he'd seen Jesus himself). What had Peter done <u>after</u> Jesus came back to life?

_____ and _____ with Jesus (v41)

Now that Peter understood that the news about Jesus was for non-Jews too, he got busy being a **chatterbox** about Jesus.

Circle the people who can't be told about Jesus...

That's right—the message about Jesus is for **EVERYONE**.

PRAY Thank God for the people who tell <u>you</u> about Jesus.

PETE KEEPS SPEAKING

Acts
10v42-43

Peter is being a chatterbox about Jesus. Use the **arrow code** to check what he has said about Jesus so far...

➡ ⬆ ↘ ↘ ⬇ ⬈

Jesus was _ _ _ _ _ _

⬆ ↘ ⬆ △ ⬇

Jesus is _ _ _ _ _ **again!**

Now read the rest of Peter's speech...

READ
Acts 10v42-43

God commanded Peter to be a chatterbox about Jesus (v42). Use **morse code** to discover two things Peter was to tell people about Jesus.

•‒‒‒ / •••‒ / ‒••‒ / ‒‒•‒ / •

Jesus is our ___ ___ ___ ___ ___ (v42)

•‒• / • / •••‒ / ‒•‒• / •• / • / •‒•

Jesus is our ___ ___ ___ ___ ___ ___ ___ (v43)

To find out more read **Ready To Be Rescued?** on the next page.

PRAY

Father God, thank you that you love me so much that you sent Jesus to rescue me. Amen

READY TO BE RESCUED?

Why do we need rescuing—and **who** is the Rescuer?

Peter explains it in Acts 10v42-43.

> Jesus is the one whom God has appointed judge of the living and the dead. (v42)

This is why we need rescuing. We are <u>all</u> going to be judged. And we <u>all</u> sin.

What is Sin?

We all like to be in charge of our own lives. We do what **we** want instead of what **God** wants. This is called Sin.

Sin gets in the way between us and God. It stops us from knowing Him and stops us from being His friends. The final result of sin is death. You can see why we need to be rescued!

> All the prophets spoke about Him...

Long before Jesus was born, the prophets (God's messengers) spoke about Him. They knew God had promised to send a Rescuer, to solve the problem of sin.

How did Jesus rescue us?

At the first Easter, when Jesus was about 33 years old, He was crucified. He was nailed to a cross and left to die.

As He died, all the sins of the world (all the wrongs people had done) were put onto Jesus. He took all of our sin onto Himself, taking the punishment we deserve. He died in our place, as our Rescuer, so that we can be forgiven.

Did You Know?

Jesus died on the cross as our Rescuer—but He didn't stay dead! After three days, God brought Him back to life! Jesus is still alive today, ruling as our King.

> ...saying that everyone who believes in Him will have his sins forgiven through His name. (v43)

When Jesus died, He dealt with the problem of sin. That means that there is nothing to separate us from God any more. That's great news for you and me!

We can know God today as our Friend and King—and one day live in heaven with Him forever.

Have YOU been rescued by Jesus? Turn to the next page to find out more...

AM I A CHRISTIAN?

Not sure if you're a Christian? Then check it out below...

Christians are people who have been rescued by Jesus and follow Him as their King.

> **You can't become a Christian by trying to be good.**

That's great news, since you can't be totally good all the time!

It's about accepting what Jesus did on the cross to rescue you. To do that, you will need to **ABCD**.

A **Admit** your sin—that you do, say and think wrong things. Tell God you are sorry. Ask Him to forgive you, and to help you to change. There will be some wrong things you have to stop doing.

B **Believe** that Jesus died for you, to take the punishment for your sin; that He came back to life, and that He is still alive today.

C **Consider** the cost of living like God's friend from now on, with Him in charge. It won't be easy. Ask God to help you do this.

D **Do** something about it! In the past you've gone your own way rather than God's way. Will you hand control of your life over to Him from now on? If you're ready to ABCD, then talk to God now. The prayer will help you.

A prayer

Dear God,
I have done and said and thought things that are wrong. I am really sorry. Please forgive me. Thank you for sending Jesus to die for me. From now on, please help me to live as one of Your friends, with You in charge. Amen

> Do you remember what Peter said?—"<u>everyone</u> who believes in Jesus will have his sin forgiven" Acts 10v43

Jesus welcomes <u>everyone</u> who comes to Him. If you have put your trust in Him, He has rescued you from your sins and will help you to live for Him. That's great news!

REALLY RESCUED?

 Acts 10v44-48

Have you ever won anything?

What was it?

How could you prove to me that you won it?

 If you had a trophy or certificate you could convince me that you had won it. The trophy would be **proof**.

God had shown Peter that the good news about Jesus was for <u>everyone</u>. That's why Peter was telling Cornelius and his non-Jewish friends about Jesus. But the other <u>Jewish</u> believers weren't sure yet. So God **proved** it to them...

READ
Acts 10v44-48

SCENE FIVE

What is the proof that Cornelius and his friends really had believed in Jesus? *Use the **number code** inside the back cover.*

19 12 15 2   8 11 18 9 18 7

They were given the _ _ _ _ _ _ _ _ _ _

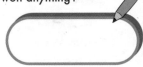

12 7 19 22 9   15 26 13 20 6 26 20 22 8

They spoke in _ _ _ _ _ _ _ _ _ _ _ _ _ _ _ _

Did You Know?

This is the same thing that happened to the Jewish believers on the Day of Pentecost. (*You can read it for yourself in **Acts 2v1-4**.*)

Peter's Jewish friends were **amazed** (v45). But this was definite proof that these non-Jews had become believers too. They were baptised and welcomed as followers of Jesus.

Peter and the others had got the point at last. The good news about Jesus really is for EVERYONE. From now on they would tell everyone (both Jews and non-Jews) all about Jesus.

PRAY

Today, the great news about Jesus has reached right around the world. Where do you live?

_____

Thank God that the great news about Jesus has reached <u>you</u> as well.

HEAVEN'S ABOVE

WELCOME TO PSALM 19!

Psalms are songs and prayers written to God. This psalm was written by King David—you know, the one who beat Goliath! In it, David tells us some top things about the universe we live in.

READ
Psalm 19v1-4

Use the **Flag Code** to find out what the sky shows us about God (v1).

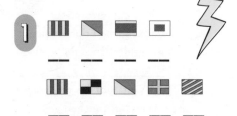

2

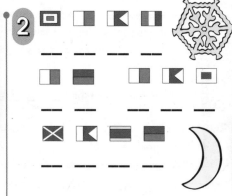

Look out of the window or go outside. What does the sky look like right now?

God made all of that! It shows us how **amazing** He is.
Sun, clouds, rain, stars, moon, lightning, snowflakes—God made it all!

READ
Psalm 19v4-6

The sun is millions of miles away. Yet it is s-o-o-o bright and powerful when it rises in the morning. God made the sun and controls it. So imagine how much more powerful **He** is!

THINK + PRAY

Look up at the sky now and tell God how great and powerful He is!
You could even try to praise God <u>every</u> time you look up and see the sun or the stars.

GOD'S GREAT WORD

We're still looking at Psalm 19—King David's song to God. Yesterday we saw how the sky shows us what God is like. *Use the Arrow Code to see what else tells us about God.*

◁ ⬈ ⬇   ⬈ ⬆ ⬈ ⬊ ⬇

_ _ _   _ _ _ _ _

READ
Psalm 19v7-11

(Circle) the words that appear in these verses.

law   teachings   commands   statutes   precepts

ordinances   judgements   instruction   rules

These all mean **God's word**—what God says to us. We read God's word in **the Bible**. So, what is God's word like? Fill in the *vowels* (a e i o u) to find out.

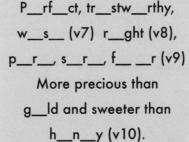

God's word is...
P__rf__ct, tr__stw__rthy,
w__s__ (v7) r__ght (v8),
p__r__, s__r__, f__ __r (v9)
More precious than
g__ld and sweeter than
h__n__y (v10).

That sounds fantastic! We should read it more often! And what does God's word **do** for us?

Gives us new str__ngth (v7)
Makes people w__s__ (v7)
Gives us j__y and
makes us h__ppy! (v8)

THINK + PRAY

God's word is perfect, pure, true, trustworthy and right. It gives joy to the heart, is more precious than gold and will last for ever! Thank God for the Bible, and ask Him to help you understand it more.

PLEASING STUFF

King David has learned loads about how great God is. Let's see how it has changed him...

READ
Psalm 19v12-13

David knows that he sometimes messes up and disobeys God. We **all** do wrong stuff, sometimes without even realising it.

From the list, tick the **wrong things** we sometimes do.

tell lies	play netball
smile lots	cheat
eat sweets	disobey parents
get angry	share things
swear	get jealous

READ
Psalm 19v14

David knows that he **says** and **thinks** wrong things. In the think bubble, write a wrong thing you've **said** or **thought** recently.

What does David do when he **does** wrong things, **says** wrong things, or **thinks** wrong thoughts?

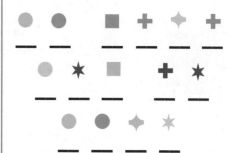

PRAY

Say sorry to God for wrong things you've done, said or thought. Ask Him to help you to <u>please Him</u> with what you do, say and think.

DAY 21 GENESIS—a book of beginnings

Earlier in **GENESIS** (and in XTB Issue One) we read about the beginnings of God's special people, the **Israelites**. We began with Abraham, and learned three things that God promised him.

Use the Flag Code to find out what they were.

As we carry on in Genesis we read about Abraham's son Isaac, and his sons. They are the next stage of the H–U–G–E family God promised to Abraham.

Here's a family tree which you can start filling in. (*Remember to come back to it when you read about other members of the family.*)

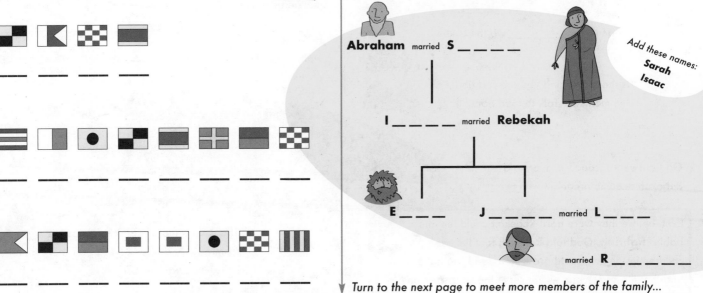

Abraham married **S _ _ _ _ _ _**

Add these names:
Sarah
Isaac

I _ _ _ _ _ _ married **Rebekah**

E _ _ _ _   **J _ _ _ _ _ _** married **L _ _ _ _**

married **R _ _ _ _ _ _**

Turn to the next page to meet more members of the family...

DOUBLE TROUBLE!

READ
Genesis 25v19-26

Isaac and Rebekah were sad because they didn't have any children. What did Isaac do? (v21)

Isaac **p**_____ to the LORD.

Is there anything <u>you</u> are sad about at the moment? Talk to God about it.

God answered Isaac's prayer, and Rebekah became pregnant with <u>twins</u>!

Even before they were born Rebekah could feel the babies **fighting**. God told Rebekah that the two children inside her would grow up to lead two nations, and that the **older** one would serve the **younger** one.

The older son was called
E _ _ _ (v25)

The younger son was called
J _ _ _ _ _ (v26)

How old was Isaac when his sons were born? (v26)

How old was Isaac when he married Rebekah? (v20)

How many years did Isaac wait for God to answer his prayer?

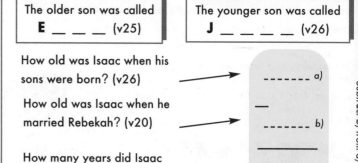

- - - - - - - a)

___

- - - - - - - b)

_____

Isaac knew that God had promised his dad (Abraham) a HUGE family. So Isaac prayed, and trusted God. And 20 years later, God kept His promise! He gave Isaac and Rebekah **two** children!

PRAY

Thank God that He always keeps His promises. (And often gives us far more than we ask for!)

DAY 22 FOOD FOR THOUGHT!

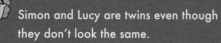

Simon and Lucy are twins even though they don't look the same.

✔ the things about them that are the same.

✘ the things about them that are different.

Mum & Dad
surnames
hobbies
birthday
first names
hair

READ
Genesis 25v27-34

Esau and Jacob were twins but they were very different. *Draw arrows to put the words inside the right person.*

loved outdoors
quiet
older
loved home
younger
Isaac's favourite
Rebekah's favourite

When Esau came in from hunting he was starving and asked Jacob for some stew. Jacob wanted something in return. *Use the **Arrow Code** to work out what it was.*

__ __ __ __ __ __ __ __ __ __

> ### Did you know?

In those days when a Father died, the older son became leader of the family and received most of the Father's belongings. This was his **BIRTHRIGHT**.

Esau cared more about **food** than his **birthright**! When Rebekah was pregnant, God told her that He had chosen to bless Jacob, rather than Esau. But Jacob was mean. He **cheated** to get what he wanted. He should have trusted God.

THINK + PRAY

It's wrong to cheat. And it's wrong not to trust God to work things out for the best. Say sorry to God for any times you have cheated. Ask Him to help you to trust Him.

THE NEXT GENERATION

 THINK SPOT

What promises have you made this week?

Have you kept them?

God had made promises to Abraham which hadn't <u>yet</u> been kept...

READ
Genesis 26v1-6

Circle the right answers.

Isaac went to the

President / King / Queen

In a place called

Germany / Jerusalem / Gerar

God told Isaac not to go to

England / Egypt / Everest

Did Isaac do what God said? (v6)

God repeated to Isaac the promises He had made to Isaac's father Abraham.

Fill in the missing letters.

1   **L _ N D** (v3)

2   **CH _ L D R _ N** (v4)

3   **B L _ S S _ N G** (v4)

God had not forgotten the **H–U–G–E** promises He had made. He reminded Isaac that He would still keep these brilliant promises.

PRAY

Isaac must have been encouraged when God told him these great things.

Thank God that He keeps His promises and that we can trust Him.

DAY 24 FAMILY FAVOURITES

xtb — Genesis 27v1-29

Isaac is now old and blind. He decides it's time to give his blessing to Esau, his eldest son.

Go hunting, and cook me a tasty meal. Then I'll give you my blessing.

But Isaac's wife Rebekah is listening in—and she has other ideas...

Jacob, I'll cook a special meal for your dad.

You can take it to him and pretend to be Esau.

But Esau's really hairy! And I'm not. What if my father touches me?

Put this goatskin on your arms and neck.

Now you feel like Esau.

Put on Esau's clothes.

Now you smell like Esau!

Go and see your father.

Who are you?

I'm Esau!

Did Jacob's trick work?
Read the passage to find out.

READ
Genesis 27v18-29

What two **lies** did Jacob tell?

v19 **"I am E_____"**

v20 **"G_____ helped me"**

THINK SPOT

This family is in a mess. They haven't lived the way God wants. Do they deserve God's blessing?

THINK + PRAY

We all make a mess of things sometimes. We don't live the way God wants us to.

Now would be a good time to say sorry for the things you've made a mess of. (Maybe you told lies like Jacob did?)

Thank God that He keeps His promises even though we don't deserve it.

DAY 25 ESAU RED!

What things make you cross or angry?

READ
Genesis 27v30-35

Use the word pool to fill in the gaps.

J_____ had pretended to be **E**_____ , so that their father would give him Esau's **B**_____ . When Esau went to his father, Isaac would **N**_____ give him the blessing. Esau became very **A**_____ and **U**_____ .

Esau

Angry

Not

Blessing

Jacob

Upset

READ
Genesis 27v41

Esau was very angry and wanted to kill Jacob.
Draw his face here.

Esau had been cheated. But it's still wrong to want revenge, however badly you've been treated.

All families have arguments but this one is **BIG!** Surely God will give up on this bunch of liars and cheats and bless someone else instead.

REMEMBER
God had chosen Jacob, but not because he was any better. God chose Jacob because He wanted to. And God's the BOSS so He's allowed to choose.

PRAY
Thank God that He's the boss—that He's in charge even when things seem to be in a mess.

DAY 26 · STRANGE DREAMS

I once tried to sleep on the concrete floor of a shed. What's the strangest place you've had to sleep? _____

Esau wanted to **kill** Jacob. So Jacob left home. He set off for Haran, to stay with his Uncle Laban...

READ
Genesis 28v10-22

Did you know?

Jacob called this place Bethel, which means **House of God**.

Jacob set off for Haran. No →
Yes ↓

Jacob had a dream. Yes →
No ↓

He stopped at sunrise. No ↑
Yes ↓

Jacob used a stone for a pillow. Yes ↑
No ↓

In it he saw Abraham. Yes ↓ No ↓

No ↑ Yes ↑

The Lord promised to be with Jacob wherever he went.

The Lord said he would leave Jacob.

The Lord promised Jacob land, children and blessing. Yes ↓

The Lord spoke to Jacob. ← Yes No ↓

God had promised **Abraham** three things.

He repeated His promise to **Isaac**.

And now to **Jacob**. (v13-14)

God promised to be with Jacob, and bring him safely home. It's a great promise—but Jacob isn't sure yet. He wants proof first (v20) before fully trusting God.

PRAY

Do **you** find it hard to trust God completely? If so, talk to God about it, and ask Him to help you.

DAY 27 WORKING FOR WIVES

Genesis chapters 29-31

Remember the three promises God gave to Abraham, Isaac and Jacob:

- Land
- Children
- Blessing

Jacob was now 500 miles away from the **land**—but in today's story God gives him **children** and **blessing**...

When Jacob arrived in Haran to stay with his uncle Laban, he met Laban's youngest daughter Rachel. Jacob soon fell in love with her...

READ
Genesis 29v18-20

How many years work did Jacob agree to do before marrying Rachel? (v18)

_____ years

But Laban <u>cheated</u> Jacob! He made Jacob marry his older daughter **Leah** first!!

So Jacob ended up with **two wives** —Rachel <u>and</u> Leah.

Add Leah and Rachel to the family tree on Day 21.

Spot six differences between these sheep.

Jacob's job was to look after Laban's sheep. Laban agreed to pay Jacob by giving him any sheep that were spotted or streaked.

(In fact, Laban kept trying to cheat Jacob—but **God** made sure that Jacob's flocks grew and grew. You can read the story in Genesis 31v4-9.)

READ
Genesis 30v43

Jacob spent 20 years with Laban. At the end he was rich. He also had **two** wives, and **eleven** sons!

This was part of God's

25	15	22	8	8	18	13	20
__	__	__	__	__	__	__	__

Use the Number Code

God gave Jacob **children** and **blessing**. He kept His promise to Jacob, even when Jacob didn't deserve it.

PRAY

Thank God that He is faithful and keeps His promises even when we don't deserve it.

DAY 28 SENDING MESSAGES

Which of these do you use to keep in touch with people?

Circle your answers

READ
Genesis 32v3-5

Jacob is on his way home. He is worried that even after 20 years Esau will still want to kill him. So Jacob sends a message. *Fill in the gaps.*

I've been staying with _____.
I now have _____, _____,
_____, _____ and
_____. I'm sending this message
in the hope of finding _____.

favour

5

cattle

Laban

servants

donkeys sheep

goats

READ
Genesis 32v6-12

Esau is coming to meet Jacob and he has **400** men with him!

Jacob is afraid.
What does he do? (v9)

He p_____

Genesis 32v1-12

THINK SPOT
For the first time Jacob admits that he **doesn't deserve** the kindness and faithfulness that God has shown him (v10), and he asks God to save him.

Jacob then chose gifts for Esau, because he wanted to make peace with him. *We'll find out more on Day 30.*

THINK + PRAY

Read v10 again.

Jacob's prayer is a good example for us to follow. We don't deserve God's kindness and faithfulness, but He is <u>always</u> kind and faithful to us. Thank God for the good things He has given you. (*Family, friends, a home...*)

DAY 29 NIGHT FIGHT

The story so far...
Before Jacob was even born, God promised to bless him.

DAY 21

But instead of trusting God to keep that promise, we've seen Jacob lying and cheating to get what he wants.

DAY 22 DAY 24

But now it's time for Jacob to admit that **God** is in charge. He needs God's help. He needs God to bless him.

Time for a strange story...

READ
Genesis 32v22-30

What a story! Jacob wrestled with a man. All night! Finally, Jacob realised that he'd been wrestling with God!

What did Jacob ask God to do?

B_____ him. (v26)

At last Jacob seems to be admitting that **God is in charge**. He knows he needs God to bless him.

Jacob's name is changed to

— — — — —

and he is blessed.

Did you know?

Giving someone a name meant that you **ruled** them. God is showing that **He is in charge** of Jacob's life.

Jacob has **changed**. Finally he is trusting God instead of trusting himself.

God stays the **same**. He always keeps His promises.

PRAY

Sometimes we choose to trust ourselves instead of trusting God. Ask God to help you to trust Him.

REUNITED after 20 years

Genesis
33v1-20

Imagine you are about to meet someone you haven't seen for years. How might you feel?

nervous

sad   excited

worried

scared   angry

happy

Jacob and Esau haven't seen each other for 20 years. Last time they saw each other Esau wanted to **kill** Jacob.

READ
Genesis 33v1-4

What did Esau do when he saw Jacob?

Wow! Esau has changed a lot!!

Jacob had to persuade Esau to accept the gifts he had brought.

READ verse 11.

Who did Jacob say had given him everything he had? (v11)

Esau wanted Jacob and his family to come home with him to Seir. Jacob said that he would—but that he wanted to travel slowly because he had young children with him. So Esau set off home on his own.

READ
Genesis 33v16-17

What did Jacob <u>actually</u> do? (v17)

_____

Yesterday we saw how Jacob admitted that God was in charge. But Jacob hasn't stopped being a liar overnight! Yet God is still at work in Jacob's life, making Jacob into the person He wants him to be.

THINK + PRAY

When we become Christians we ask God to take charge of our lives. But we don't change straight away. Some of our old habits are still there.
Thank God that He's still at work today, making <u>you</u> into the person He wants you to be.

MORE MATTHEW

If you wrote a book, what would it be about?

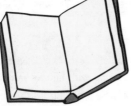

Write your answer in the book.

Matthew wrote a book about Jesus. He wanted people to know **who** Jesus is and what He came to **do**.

What a great book! Let's get started.

Wait! We've already read the beginning of Matthew in Issue One! Remember?

Umm?

Let's see what Matthew has told us about Jesus already...

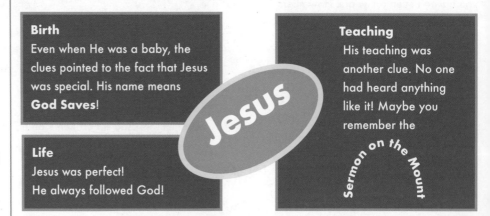

Birth
Even when He was a baby, the clues pointed to the fact that Jesus was special. His name means **God Saves!**

Life
Jesus was perfect! He always followed God!

Jesus

Teaching
His teaching was another clue. No one had heard anything like it! Maybe you remember the Sermon on the Mount

Now Matthew gives us <u>more clues</u> about **who** Jesus is and what He came to **do**. Try and spot them!

Now can we start?

Yep—start now on the next page.

THE KING'S POWER

xtb · Matthew 8v1-4

Jesus (the promised King) has been telling people what it's like to follow Him. His <u>teaching</u> amazed everyone. Now watch as Jesus shows His **power**.

READ
Matthew 8v1-4

Did the sick man believe Jesus could make him better? (v2)

Circle the right answer

Did Jesus want to make him better? (v3)

Did You Know?

Leprosy is a terrible skin disease. If you had leprosy, you had to stay away from everyone—even God! AND there was no medicine to make you better!

How long did it take Jesus to heal the man? (v3)

• About two seconds

• One week

• One year

Draw a picture of the man's face when Jesus made him better.

What great news for the man. It's also great news for us!

Why? Because it tells us Jesus is:

11 12 4 22 9 21 6 15

_ _ _ _ _ _ _ _

*Use the **Number Code** to discover the answer.*

PRAY

Thank God that the things Jesus did on earth teach us that He is powerful.

DAY 32 GREAT FAITH

 xtb | Matthew 8v5-13

Draw a line to show who has these GREAT things.

GREAT strength   Models

GREAT speed   Weightlifters

GREAT looks   Sprinters

Let's see who has GREAT faith.

READ
Matthew 8v5-10

Underline the right words.

Jesus was met by a **doctor/Roman soldier/beggar**. He wanted Jesus to heal his **wife/servant/dog**. He believed that Jesus could heal him **by going to his house/just by speaking**.

The soldier believed that Jesus could heal his servant right there, just by speaking. Was he right?

READ verse 13 to find out.

Did Jesus heal the servant? ⬭

Jesus said this faith was the GREATEST He had found. (v10)

Put the gaps between the words in the right places to find out why.

Beca use iti sin Jes us

B_____ i__ i__ i__ J_____

PRAY Ask God to give **you** faith in Jesus.

DAY 33 A PROMISING CLUE

A vase of flowers has been knocked over. Use this clue to work out who did it.

The miracles Jesus did are **clues** to tell us who He is. Let's find out some more.

READ
Matthew 8v14-16

Whose house did Jesus go to? (v14)

P_____

Who was sick? (v14)

Peter's M_____ in law.

Did Jesus heal her?

Jesus had healed her so completely that she got up and served them!

How many people did Jesus heal that evening? (v16)

some
none
all

Circle the right answer

Did You Know?

You'll find loads of Old Testament chunks in Matthew's book. They show that Jesus is the **Rescuer** who was promised by God. That's why Matthew includes a chunk from the book of Isaiah...

READ
Matthew 8v17

What do these miracles tell us about Jesus?

Find the beginning of the chain in the middle. Write down each of the letters in the spaces.

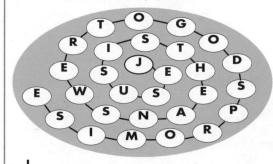

J_ _ _ _ _ _ _ _ _ _ _ _

_ _ _ _ _ _ _

_ _ _ _ _ _ _ _ _ _ _

Jesus' miracles show that He is the **Rescuer** God promised in the Old Testament.

PRAY
Thank God for keeping His promise to send Jesus.

DAY 34 FOLLOWING THE KING

Put a tick next to the things that are important to you.

- ☐ Family
- ☐ Food
- ☐ Schoolwork
- ☐ Sport
- ☐ _____

Add one of your own

For a follower of Jesus—Jesus needs to be **most** important.

READ
Matthew 8v18-22

Two people think they want to follow Jesus.

Match up the people with their speech bubbles.

A teacher of the law (v19)

Another disciple (v21)

Let me bury my Father first

I'll go wherever you go!

These people say they want to follow Jesus, but Jesus knows that He isn't the **most** important thing in their life.

Unravel the words in the pictures to see what is more important to them than Jesus.

HSOUE

A nice **H**_____

FAIMLY

F_____

THINK + PRAY

Circle the things that can become more important to you than Jesus.

friends

homework

family

sport

money

Ask God to help you to put Him first, even if it means giving something up.

DAY 35 FLOUNDERING FAITH

One of my earliest memories is getting caught in a storm with my Mum. We had to shelter in someone's garage!

READ
Matthew 8v23-25

Where were Jesus and His friends when they got caught in a storm? (v24)

In a _____ on a _____

Imagine being caught in such a strong storm!

What was Jesus doing? (v24)

S_____

Jesus was sleeping, but the disciples weren't so calm. They were very scared. They thought the boat might sink!

Draw their faces:

 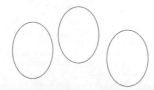

READ
Matthew 8v26-27

Circle the right answer

Did they need to be scared?   **Yes**   **No**

They didn't need to be scared because Jesus could stop the storm. But they didn't realise **who** Jesus was.

Use the **Arrow Code** to find out the next clue Matthew gives us about Jesus.

Jesus is more __ __ __ __ __ __ __ __ than

anything in the __ __ __ __ __

PRAY

Thank God that Jesus is more powerful than anything you are scared of, and that we can trust Him.

DAY 36 WHO IS THIS MAN?

<u>Underline</u> the things or people that obey you.

Friends   Pets
Little brothers/sisters
Weather

READ
Matthew 8v27

What obeys Jesus?

The **w**_____ and the **w**_____

Let's find out for them!
Read these lines from the Old Testament.

> LORD God Almighty, none is as mighty as you; in all things you are faithful, O LORD. You rule over the powerful sea; you calm its angry waves.
>
> Psalm 89v8-9

Only <u>God</u> could calm a storm, because He is in charge of everything.

Read along the wave to answer the people's question:

Jesus is God

Jesus stopped a storm just by speaking! No wonder everyone was amazed!

What were they all asking? (v27)

W_____ k_____ of
m_____ is t_____ ?

this
kind what
man

THINK + PRAY

When our friends say that Jesus was just a man, how can we show that He is God?
(E.g. tell them about the things Jesus can **do**.)

Ask God to help you tell your friends about Jesus.

DAY 37 DEMON DESTROYER

 Matthew 8v28-34

What does Jesus show power over in today's story?

*Use the **Flag Code***

— — — — — — — —

READ
Matthew 8v28

How many men met Jesus?
Circle the right picture

What did the two men have in them? (v28)

D_____

Demons are evil spirits; they are God's enemies. How did the demons make the men behave? (v28)

 Cross out the wrong answer

Fierce and violent   Calm and gentle

READ
Matthew 8v29-34

What did the demons call Jesus? (v29)

S_____ of G_____

The demons knew who Jesus was. They knew He was far more powerful than them. When Jesus told them to leave they had to obey.

That's great news! *Follow the arrows to find out why:*

and the → than evil

got better. ←   Jesus is

two men   more powerful

THINK SPOT Some people <u>didn't</u> think it was good news. They were cross because their pigs had died! Do <u>you</u> let unimportant things become more important than Jesus?

PRAY   Thank God that Jesus has power over evil.

SIN DESTROYER

The clues we've looked at show Jesus is the promised Rescuer and He's God. But what did He come to **do**? Let's find out!

READ
Matthew 9v1-2

Who met Jesus? (v2)

Some p_____ carrying a p_____ man.

The paralysed man couldn't move at all. Imagine if **you** couldn't move—what would the worst thing be?

Jesus wanted to solve the man's BIGGEST problem.

What did Jesus say to the paralysed man? (v2)

Your sins are forgiven	You can move now
☐	☐

✔ *the right answer.*

Use the first letter of each picture to discover the problem Jesus came to solve.

Did You Know?

Everyone's biggest problem is **sin**. Sin is doing what **we** want instead of what **God** wants. Sin separates us from God.

THINK + PRAY Did you realise your BIGGEST problem is sin? Say sorry to God for your sin and thank Him that Jesus came to <u>solve</u> the problem of sin.

DAY 39 GET UP AND GO

The story so far...
Some men brought their paralysed friend to Jesus. Jesus told the man that his **sins** were forgiven.

Sin is a problem **only** God can solve. Jesus wants people to know that He is God and He has come to forgive sin.

READ
Matthew 9v3

Did the teachers of the law believe Jesus? (v3)

Colour the right answer

No

Yes

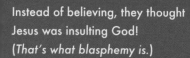

Instead of believing, they thought Jesus was insulting God!
(*That's what blasphemy is.*)

READ
Matthew 9v4-8

What did Jesus say to the paralysed man? (v6)

G_____ u___ !

It seems a strange thing to say to someone who can't move! But what happened to the man? (v7)

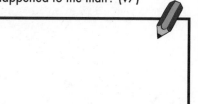

What did Jesus prove by healing him? (v6) *Use **Morse Code** to find out*

He could

·–··/–·–/··–/––/··/·····–/

__ __ __ __ __ __ __

···/··/–··/···

__ __ __ __

The teachers of the law were wrong! Jesus **is** God and He **can** forgive sins.

PRAY

Dear God, help me believe that Jesus has the power to forgive sins.

DAY 40 JESUS' FRIENDS

Who are your friends?

Write down their names
- _____
- _____
- _____

Today we read about Jesus making some new friends.

READ
Matthew 9v9

Circle the right answers.

Jesus met a man called **Peter / Matthew / Sam**. This man was a **doctor / tax collector / fisherman**. Jesus told the man to **follow Him / go away**. The man got up and **went away / followed Jesus**.

Booo!

No-one really liked tax collectors —they were often liars and cheats.

But Jesus wanted to be **friends** with Matthew!

Huh?

READ
Matthew 9v10-11

The religious leaders thought this was terrible! They thought Jesus should only spend time with **good** people.

READ
Matthew 9v12-13

xtb Matthew 9v9-13

Draw a line from the doctor to the person he helps.

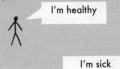

I'm healthy

I'm sick

Imagine a doctor never spending time with sick people! It would be even worse if Jesus didn't make friends with people who need His forgiveness.

Who needs forgiveness? *Write down all the red letters to find out.*

_ _ _ _ _ _ _ _ _

PRAY

Thank God that Jesus came to make friends with people who need His forgiveness, including you and me.

TIME TO PARTY!

 Matthew 9v14-15

 Did You know?

People **fasted** (went without food) because they were sad about sin and wanted God to sort the problem out.

Circle the people who are _fasting_.

READ
Matthew 9v14-15

What was different about Jesus' disciples? (v14)

They didn't **f_____**

Who does Jesus compare the disciples to? (v15)

People enjoying a wedding party with the groom	

✔ the right answer

 Sad people | |

Circle the people who are _partying_.

When Jesus came it was time for celebrating—not being sad!
Read around the balloon to find out why.

He came to solve the problem of sin once and for all

All through the Old Testament God prepared His people for Jesus. But when Jesus arrived, not many people celebrated. Sadly, they wanted to keep going as if Jesus hadn't come. That's like looking forward to a party but never going to it!

THINK + PRAY

What about you? Are you ready to change because of what you learn about Jesus? Ask God's help.

DAY 42 **DEATH DEFYING**

xtb — Matthew 9v18-26

1

We've seen that Jesus has power over **evil**, **sickness** and **weather**.
Find the underlined words in the wordsearch. Some are written backwards!

D	E	L	I	V	E	A	T
W	E	A	T	H	E	R	H
S	S	E	N	K	C	I	S

Copy the leftover letters (in order) to see what else Jesus has power over.

_ _ _ _ _

2

READ
Matthew 9v18-19

What happened to the man's daughter? (v18)

Circle the right answer ➡ She was ill

She had died

What did the man believe Jesus could do? (v18)

3

READ
Matthew 9v23-26

See how upset everyone was—she had definitely died. But how does Jesus describe her? (v24)

Jesus knew she was dead. He also knew He would bring her back to life as easy as waking her up!

Did they believe Him? (v24) **Yes** **No** Circle the right answer

4

Did Jesus bring the girl back to life? (v25)

Wow! This is another clue that Jesus is God—and that He can solve the problem of sin.

THINK + PRAY

Do you believe in Jesus' power like the girl's father did? Ask God to help you.

DAY 43 HELP!

Write the letter in the circle with the matching colour to see what today's lesson is about.

H F I A T ◯ ◯ ◯ ◯ ◯

Last time, Jesus brought a little girl back to life. Today we find out what happened on the way to her house...

READ
Matthew 9v20-22

Who came up behind Jesus? (v20)

Circle the right answer

How long had the woman been ill? (v20)

3 years   6 years   12 years

Wow! That's probably longer than you've been alive!

How did she think she could get better? (v21)

cloak
touching

By t_____ Jesus' c_____

Follow the lines to see what was important ✔ about what she did and what wasn't important ✘

✘ ——— **Touching** Jesus

✔ ——— **Believing** Jesus could help her

Jesus wanted the woman to understand this.

What did He say? (v22)

> Your f_____ has made you well.

Faith is **believing** Jesus can help us.

PRAY

Dear God, thank you that Jesus can help me. Help me to have faith in Jesus. Amen

FAITH OR DISBELIEF?

In today's story, two blind men have realised who Jesus is from all the clues. *Use the* **Flag Code** *to see what they call Jesus.*

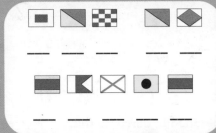

READ
Matthew 9v27-31

Son of David was another name for God's promised Rescuer. The blind men realised who Jesus was—that's why they were sure He could heal them. **And He did!**

READ
Matthew 9v32-34

What was wrong with the man they brought to Jesus? (v32)

He couldn't t_____

Why couldn't he talk? (v32)

Because of a d_____
(an evil spirit, God's enemy)

Jesus healed the man.
What was he able to do now?

Jesus showed He had **great power**.

Draw lines to show who said what about Jesus' power (v33,34)

Pharisees

crowds

Wow! We've never seen anything like this!

Jesus is bad.

THINK + PRAY

The Pharisees didn't realise who Jesus was. The blind men did. What is **your** reaction to what you've read about Jesus?

Ask God to help you believe the truth about Jesus

SPREAD THE NEWS

xtb — Matthew 9v35-38

READ
Matthew 9v35

Match the puzzle pieces to see what Jesus did.

Taught	every sickness
Preached	in synagogues
Healed	the good news

Jesus showed His power in words **and** actions to help people see why He came.

Do you remember why He came?

Use a mirror to find out

| niz ʇo məlqorq əɥʇ əvloz oʇ |

READ
Matthew 9v36-38

How did Jesus describe the crowds? (v36)

Cross out the wrong answers

helpless

relaxed   no problems

sheep without a shepherd

The people had a great need. **They needed Jesus.**

He also says they are like a harvest ready to be collected (v37). What do you think Jesus means?

a) They enjoy sunshine
b) They are ready to hear about Him
c) They look like wheat

If they are ready to hear—**people need to tell them** about Jesus.

THINK + PRAY

Who could you tell about Jesus?
_____
Pray for God to use you to tell people about Jesus.

PROMISE LAND

So far in the book of Genesis we've met...

Abraham

his son **Isaac**

and his grandson **Jacob**

God made the same three promises to all of them:

1 ✦ ■ ★ ■
___ ___ ___ ___

2 ■ ● ✦ ✦ ■ ★ ● ★
_____

3 ■ ✦ ● ✛ ✛ ✦ ★ ●
_____

GENESIS—a book of beginnings

In chapter 37 of Genesis, Jacob is living in the **land** God has promised. God has **blessed** him and made him rich. And Jacob has 13 **children**!

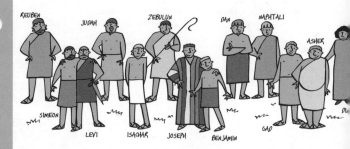

REUBEN JUDAH ZEBULUN DAN NAPHTALI ASHER
SIMEON LEVI ISACHAR JOSEPH BENJAMIN GAD

But God hasn't finished keeping His promises yet. There's more to come.

The rest of the book of Genesis tells us what happened next. It's mainly about one of Jacob's sons—**Joseph**.

Find out more on the next page →

HAPPY FAMILIES?

 Genesis 37v1-11

Joseph and his brothers are looking after their dad's sheep. They look like a happy family. But are they? Let's listen in and see...

READ
Genesis 37v1-4

Cross out the wrong words.

Joseph was **15 / 17 / 19** years old. He and his brothers looked after their father's **shells / ships / sheep**. Joseph told his dad a **bad / good** report about his brothers. Jacob loved Joseph the best. He gave Joseph a special **wig / bag / robe**. Joseph's brothers **loved / hated** Joseph.

Joseph had two dreams which made his brothers hate him even more...

READ
Genesis 37v5-11

Joseph's first dream was about sheaves of corn. *Draw what he saw.* (v7)

What did Joseph see in his second dream? (v9)

Joseph's brothers knew what his dream meant. It meant he would <u>rule</u> over them all. How did they feel? (v11)

 This is <u>not</u> a happy family! And **THINK SPOT** things are going to get worse! But there's also a hint in Joseph's dreams about what will happen in the future.

God has made HUGE promises to this family. It won't always <u>look</u> like it—but no matter what happens in Joseph's story, **God** is always in charge. He is going to keep His promises.

PRAY **Thank God that He always keeps His promises.**

DAY 47 RESCUE REQUIRED

Can you rescue Zoe from the maze?

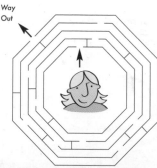

Way Out

GOD'S RESCUE PLAN

Jacob's family need to be rescued—but they don't know that yet! A famine is coming to their land. The food will run out, and they will starve if they stay there. But God has a plan to **rescue** them.

Who will God use to rescue Jacob's family?

Use the Arrow Code

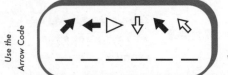

– – – – – –

JOSEPH'S PROBLEM

Joseph has a problem of his own. His brothers **hate** him. When Jacob sends Joseph to visit his brothers, they see the chance to get rid of him for ever...

READ
Genesis 37v18-20

What did Joseph's brothers plan to do? (v18)

K_____ Joseph

REUBEN'S RESCUE PLAN

Reuben was Joseph's oldest brother. He wanted to save Joseph...

READ
Genesis 37v21-24

Reuben plans to rescue Joseph, and take him back to _____ (v22)

God has a rescue plan. So does Reuben! Will the plans work?
We'll find out tomorrow...

THINK SPOT

The main point of this story is <u>God's Rescue Plan for His people</u>. But it's worth noticing some other stuff that's going on too. This family is in a **mess**. Joseph is Jacob's favourite son. Joseph's brothers are very jealous. They end up hating Joseph.

THINK + PRAY

Do you have any brothers or sisters? Do you ever feel like you **hate** them? Maybe you're **jealous** of them?

Ask God to help you to **love** the people in your family—even when that's really hard.

DAY 48 MAN WITH A PLAN

Yesterday we found out about **three plans**:

1 God's plan to use Joseph to <u>rescue</u> Jacob's family.

2 Joseph's brothers' wicked plan to <u>kill</u> Joseph.

3 Reuben's plan to <u>save</u> Joseph from his brothers.

We left Joseph at the bottom of a dry well.
Let's find out what happened next...

READ
Genesis 37v25-28

(Circle your answers.)

What did the brothers see? (v25)

What did they decide? (v26)

| Let's kill him! | Let's tickle him! | Let's sell him! |

What did they sell Joseph for? (v28)

Instead of killing Joseph, his brothers sold him as a slave. Their plan was <u>changed</u>.

Reuben wasn't there when Joseph was sold. When he got back it was too late. His rescue plan had <u>failed</u>!

The brothers took Joseph's special robe and covered it in goat's blood. Then they gave the robe to their father. Jacob wept when he saw it. He believed that Joseph was dead. (*If you have time, read this bit for yourself in verses 29-35.*)

READ verse 36

Joseph was now in **E_____**
— which was just where God needed him to be!

THINK + PRAY

The brothers' plan was <u>changed</u>. Reuben's plan <u>failed</u>. But God's plan was working out just as He intended. God's plans always do!
Thank God that His good plans never fail.

BAD NEWS GOOD NEWS

Genesis 39v1-23

The **good news** is—I bought you a bag of sweets.

The **bad news** is—I ate them on the way home!

BAD NEWS

Potiphar's wife fancied Joseph. Even though she was married, she kept asking Joseph to go to bed with her.

BAD NEWS
Potiphar's wife was furious. She lied about Joseph to get him into trouble. Potiphar believed his wife. Even though Joseph had done nothing wrong, he was thrown into **prison**.

BAD NEWS
Joseph has been sold by his brothers. Now he's a **slave**, working for an important Egyptian official called Potiphar.

READ
Genesis 39v7-10

READ
Genesis 39v19-23

READ
Genesis 39v1-6

GOOD NEWS
Joseph said **NO!** He told Potiphar's wife it would be a sin because he would be disobeying God.

GOOD NEWS
Who was with Joseph? (v21)
God gave Joseph success in everything he did. The prison warder put Joseph **in charge** of everything.

GOOD NEWS
Who was with Joseph? (v2)
God gave Joseph success in everything he did. So Potiphar put Joseph **in charge** of everything.

THINK SPOT

Sometimes people want us to do stuff that we know is wrong. When that happens we need to say **NO!**, just like Joseph did. **Ask God to help you.**

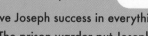
PRAY Look back at the Think Spot. Ask God to help you to be like Joseph.

DAY 50 DREAM JOB

xtb Genesis 40v1-15

Joseph was still in prison. But it wasn't an ordinary prison—it was where the <u>king's</u> prisoners were sent.

One day, the king (Pharaoh) threw two men into prison. They were his cupbearer (who tested the king's wine) and his royal baker. After they'd been there quite a while, they both had dreams...

READ
Genesis 40v6-8

The two men didn't understand their dreams. Who did Joseph say <u>can</u> explain dreams? (v8)

G_____

The cupbearer told Joseph his dream. *Fill in the missing bits in the pictures.*

I saw a vine with three branches.

It grew leaves and flowers.

Then it grew many bunches of grapes.

I squeezed the grapes into the king's cup, and gave it to him.

God showed Joseph what the dream meant.

READ
Genesis 40v12-15

What great news—in three days the cupbearer would be set free! What did Joseph ask him to do? (v14)

R_____ me.

Joseph <u>didn't deserve</u> to be in prison. But God was going to use him to <u>rescue</u> his family from the coming famine.
Does that remind you of someone else?

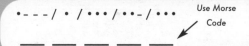
Use Morse Code

PRAY Jesus never did anything wrong. But He was arrested and killed to <u>rescue</u> us from our sins. Thank God for sending Jesus to be our Rescuer.

*Check out **Ready to be Rescued** after Day 16 if you want to know more.*

The cupbearer dreamed about **vines** and **grapes**. The baker's dream was about **bread** and **cakes**. *Spot eight differences in the two pictures.*

READ
Genesis 40v16-19

In the cupbearer's dream, it was the <u>king</u> who drank from the cup. But what ate the bread and cakes in the baker's dream? (v17)

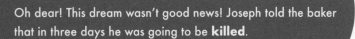

Oh dear! This dream wasn't good news! Joseph told the baker that in three days he was going to be **killed**.

Joseph had told both men what their dreams meant. But was he right? *Read the verses to find out.*

READ
Genesis 40v20-22

Was the cupbearer set free from prison? (v21)

Was the baker killed? (v22)

It all happened **exactly** as God had told Joseph. What God says **always** comes true.

PRAY **Thank God that His words always come true.**

Joseph had asked the cupbearer to help him get out of prison (v14). But sneak a peek at **verse 23**.

Joseph is going to stay in prison a bit longer...

TWO YEARS TOO MANY?

Genesis 41v1-16

How old will you be in **two years** time?

How will you be different by then? (eg: taller, in a new class at school, new friends...)

Joseph spent **two more years** in prison. And all because the cupbearer had forgotten him! (Or was it?? Those extra two years meant that Joseph came out of prison at **just the right time**. It was all part of God's plan!)

READ
Genesis 41v1-8

Pharaoh didn't understand his dreams, so he sent for "*all the wise men and magicians in Egypt.*" (v8).

 Could they tell him what the dreams meant? (v8) ✔ ✘

Then the cupbearer remembered Joseph. (After two years!) He told Pharaoh all about him.

Pharaoh sent for Joseph right away. He wanted Joseph to explain his dreams. But look what Joseph said...

_ _ _   _ _   _ _ _ _ _ _ _

Wow! Was Joseph refusing to help the king? *Read the verses to find out.*

READ
Genesis 41v14-16

Joseph knew that only <u>one</u> person could explain Pharaoh's dream. Who? (v16)

 G_____

Joseph knew that on his own he would be no more successful than all the wise men and magicians who had tried before. But he was sure that **God** would show him what Pharaoh's dream meant.

THINK + PRAY

Are there things you <u>want</u> to do, but <u>can't</u>? (eg: *Always being truthful, sharing with people you don't like, thinking of others before yourself...*) Ask <u>God</u> to help you with these things.

DAY 53 COWS AND CORN

Genesis 41v17-36

Pharaoh told Joseph his dreams...

READ
Genesis 41v17-24

Spot the mistakes in Pharaoh's dreams. There are **ten** to find. Circle each one.

I was standing on the Bank of England, when out of the river came seven windmills. They were short and fat. Then eight more cows came up. They were thin and beautiful. The thin cows kissed the fat cows—but looked just as bad as before. I also dreamed about seven fingers of corn, growing on one stalk. Then seven thin ears of corn sprouted. They had been scorched by a barbecue. The thin corn painted the fat corn. I told my dreams to the clowns, but they couldn't explain them.

Joseph told Pharaoh that both dreams meant the same thing.

READ
Genesis 41v28-33

Joseph told Pharaoh four things:

• There will be plenty of food for _____ years.

• Then there will seven years of _____ .

• God will definitely do this. He will do it _____ .

• You need a put a _____ man in charge of the land.

wise

famine

soo

seven

God made His message **very clear**. He warned Pharaoh what would happen—and told him how to solve the problem. Would Pharaoh listen? We'll find out tomorrow!

THINK + PRAY

Sometimes, even though God's words are **very clear**, we don't do what He says. For example:
Give to those in need. (Matthew 6v3)
Forgive those who hurt you. (Matthew 18v21-22)
Tell others about Jesus. (Matthew 28v19-20)
Do you find it hard to do what God says? Then ask Him to help you.

Answers: The mistakes are—England, windmills, short, eight, beautiful, kissed, fingers, barbecue, painted, clowns.

DAY 54 TOP JOB

Pharaoh needed a man to help Egypt get ready for the famine. He chose **Joseph**—just as God had planned.

READ
Genesis 41v39-40

Wow! Look how God's plans were working out. Joseph was now second-in-command of the whole country!

During the next seven years, Joseph collected l-o-a-d-s of food and stored it in the cities of Egypt. There was so much that Joseph stopped counting it!

Joseph also got married, and had two sons. Use the Shape Code to discover their names.

Look out for the meaning of these names as you read the verses.

READ
Genesis 41v50-52

In Bible times, names were often chosen because of their meaning. These names reminded Joseph that **God** was with him.

Pharaoh knew that God was with Joseph.

G_____ has shown you all this. (v39)

So did Joseph...

G_____ has made me forget all my sufferings. (v51)

G_____ has made me fruitful, and given me children. (v52)

THINK + PRAY

Joseph knew that everything he had came from God. The Bible tells us that everything we have comes from God too.

Think of **three things** you can thank God for. Then do it!

Follow the path through today's page!

The famine was everywhere. Jacob's family were running out of food.

Jacob sent ten of his sons to Egypt to buy grain. But he kept the youngest, Benjamin, safe at home.

The brothers arrived in Egypt. They came to Joseph to ask for grain—but they didn't recognise him!

If you have time, read the whole story in v1-17

READ
Genesis 42v6-11

Joseph decided to test his brothers. "You are **s**_____", he said (v9). Then he threw them into prison!

When the brothers bowed down before Joseph, he remembered his **d**_____ (v9).
We read about them on Day 46.

The brothers spent three days in prison.
We'll find out what happens to them tomorrow.

PRAY Think of some countries where there is famine right now. Pray for the starving people there, and for those who are helping them. Can you help in any other way?

Stop here until tomorrow— when we'll find out what happens to Joseph's brothers...

DAY 56 ...AND BACK AGAIN

But Jacob refused to let them take Benjamin back to Egypt.

Will Simeon be stuck in Egypt for ever? What will Jacob do when the food runs out? More tomorrow...

PRAY

The brothers didn't understand what was happening, but they were right to think that **God** was in charge. (v28) Thank God that He is <u>always</u> in control.

When the brothers got home, they told Jacob everything that had happened.

What has **G_____** done to us? (v28)

On the way home, they opened a sack of **g_____**, and found **s_____** inside it! (v27) They were scared!

READ

Genesis 42v23-28

After three days, Joseph let his brothers out of prison.

He told them they could go back home—on two conditions:
1. They leave one brother (**Simeon**) in prison in Egypt.
2. They bring **Benjamin** back with them.

The brothers agreed—and headed for home.

DAY 57 TO EGYPT (again!)

xtb Genesis 43v1 - 44v17

The food had run out again. Jacob's sons had to return to Egypt, where Simeon was still stuck in prison. But this time they must take Benjamin with them, as Joseph had commanded (Genesis 42v34).

You can read the whole story in Genesis 43v1-44v17

Send Benjamin with me. I promise to look after him

EGYPT

The brothers were scared—but Joseph gave them lunch!

Look! He's put us in order from the oldest to the youngest!

How does he know???

Give them as much food as they can carry.

But hide my silver cup in the youngest one's sack!

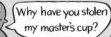

The brothers left—but Joseph sent his steward after them.

Why have you stolen my master's cup?

We've done nothing wrong!

Search us and see!

But the cup was found...

in Benjamin's sack!

The brothers all returned to see Joseph. What would he say?

READ
Genesis 44v14-17

Oh no! Judah said they would all stay as slaves—but Joseph said only one of them must become his slave. Who? (v17)

B_____

PRAY

What a mess! It looks like a disaster—but as we'll see, it all works out in God's way.
Ask God to help you to keep trusting Him—even when life seems to be in a mess.

20 years had passed since Joseph was sold by his brothers. The question was—had they changed in that time?

Spot six differences in these pictures of Joseph's brother Judah.

Younger Judah

Older Judah

Judah and his brothers had all changed on the <u>outside</u>. But had they changed on the <u>inside</u> too? Or were they just as cruel as ever?

Read what Judah said to Joseph.

READ

Genesis 44v30-34

Did you know?

20 years before, it was **Judah** who had the idea to sell Joseph as a slave! (*That story is in Genesis 37v26-28.*)

But Judah had **changed**.
Fill in the speech bubbles.

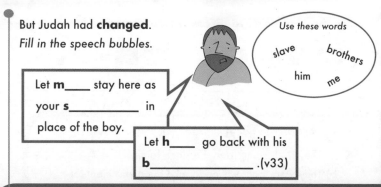

Use these words

slave   brothers   him   me

Let **m**____ stay here as your **s**_____ in place of the boy.

Let **h**____ go back with his **b**_____ .(v33)

Wow! What a H—U—G—E change! Judah is willing to be a slave for the rest of his life, so that Benjamin can go home.

THINK + PRAY

Judah had been cruel and unloving—but God had changed him.
If we are followers of Jesus, then God will change us too—to become more like Jesus.

Think carefully: Do you want God to change you? In what ways? Talk to God about your answer.

DAY 59 FAMILY LIKENESS

xtb Genesis 49v10

Use the Flag Code to discover two names.

_ _ _ _ _   _ _ _ _ _

Judah was willing to take the punishment for someone else. He was ready to become a slave so that Benjamin could go free.

How are these two people linked? (*Tick your answers.*)

a) They both come from the same family.
b) They were both willing to take the punishment for someone else.
c) Their names both begin with **J**!

Actually, all three are true!

Skip ahead to chapter 49 to see what Jacob said when he gave his final blessing to Judah.

Judah was like **Jesus** when he did this. When did Jesus take the punishment for someone else?
Write your answer here.

Read **Ready to be Rescued** after Day 16 to check your answer.

READ
Genesis 49v10

A *sceptre* is a pole carried by a king. Jacob was saying that someone from Judah's family would be <u>king for ever</u>. That person is **Jesus**!

PRAY **Thank God for sending Jesus to take the punishment for your sin, so that you can be forgiven.**

DAY 60 SURPRISE SURPRISE!

 Genesis 45v1-15

Joseph
- sold by his brothers
- served as a slave
- sentenced to prison
- saved by a dream
- second-in-command to the king

*And now Joseph tells his brothers that this was underlined all part of **God's Plan**!*

But first, Joseph has to tell them who he really is! How do you think they will feel when they find out Joseph is alive?

READ
Genesis 45v1-3

How did the brothers react? (v3)

Circle your answers

unable to speak   dancing for joy

happy

pleased to see him   terrified

Joseph told his brothers not to worry.

READ
Genesis 45v4-8

Use the Pig Pen code.

God sent me here to

∨ ⌐ > □

_ _ _ _ lives. (v5)

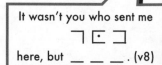

It wasn't you who sent me

⌐ ⊡ ⌐

here, but _ _ _. (v8)

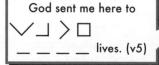

Wow! All those ups and downs in Joseph's life were really for the good of him and his family. Just as God planned.

Then Joseph gave his brothers a message for his father (it's in v9-11), and he urged them to bring Jacob to Egypt as soon as possible.

THINK + PRAY

Romans 8v28 says, "In underlined all things God works for the underlined good of those who underlined love Him."

Think carefully about the underlined words. Then thank God that He is like this.

DAY 61   ONE TWO THREE

Today we're going to think backwards! (*A mirror will help if you get stuck.*)

What were the three promises God gave to Abraham, Isaac and Jacob?

1 Land   L_____
2 Children   C_____
3 Blessing   B_____

THREE   (BLESSING)

Did you know?

Someone from Jacob's family would be God's way of <u>blessing</u> the whole world.

Who?   Jesus   J_____

If this promise was going to come true, God had to save Jacob's family from the famine. Who did God use to rescue them?   Joseph   J_____

OWT   (CHILDREN)

Jacob had 13 <u>children</u>. But for 20 years he'd believed that Joseph was dead. Now he'd sent the rest of his sons to Egypt for food. Maybe he'd never see any of them again!

READ
Genesis 45v25-28

What did Jacob's sons tell him? (v26)

Joseph is still alive!	Joseph is still _____

What fantastic news! Joseph was alive. He was waiting in Egypt—where there was plenty of food for Jacob's family, <u>and</u> they'd been promised the best of the land to live in! (*Pharaoh made this promise in 45v18*)

But there's a problem...

xtb   Genesis 45v25 - 46v7

ONE   (LAND)

God had promised to give Jacob's family a <u>land</u> of their own. But that land wasn't Egypt—it was **Canaan**.

READ
Genesis 46v1-7

What did God tell Jacob? (v4)

I will go with you.	I _____

PRAY

God promised to be <u>with</u> Jacob in Egypt—and to bring his family safely <u>back</u> to Canaan. God made sure that His promises would come true. Thank God that <u>nothing</u> can make Him break His promises.

DAY 62 CAVE MAN

The story so far...

Jacob's sons came safely back from Egypt. They had amazing news!

> Joseph is alive!

Jacob and his family left Canaan to go to Egypt. On the way, **God** spoke to Jacob.

> I will go with you.

Jacob's family settled in Goshen —the best land in Egypt.

> Let them live in Goshen.

Did you know?

Jacob was **130** years old when he moved to Egypt. He died there **17** years later. How old was he when he died? _____

Just before he died, Jacob called all his sons together. First he spoke of what would happen to them in the future. (*We read Jacob's words to Judah on Day 59.*) Then Jacob told his sons where they were to bury him.

READ
Genesis 49v29-33

Jacob wanted to be buried in a **c_____** . His grandad **A_____**, his dad **I_____** and their wives were all buried there too. The cave was in the country of **C_____** —the land God had promised to give to Jacob's family. Jacob was sure God would keep that promise.

> Isaac
> Abraham
> cave
> Canaan

THINK SPOT

Verse 33 ends with some odd words: "*Jacob was gathered to his people.*" "His people" means Jacob's dad Isaac, his grandad Abraham—and other people like them. People who **loved** and **trusted** God.

THINK + PRAY

Jacob knew that dying wasn't the <u>end</u> for him! He would be in heaven with God. *Do you worry about dying?* If we love and trust Jesus, we don't need to be scared of dying. We know that we will be with Him in heaven for ever! *How does that make you feel?* Talk to God about it.

Answer: Jacob was 147 years old when he died.

DAY 63 SOB STORY

Jacob had died. His sons were sad—but they were also worried!

> What if Joseph wants to pay us back for everything we did to him?

So they sent a message to Joseph. They told him Jacob had said that Joseph must forgive his brothers.

READ
Genesis 50v15-17

What did Joseph do when he heard his brothers' message? (v17)

Joseph _____

Draw his face

Then Joseph's brothers came to see him.

READ
Genesis 50v18-21

Fill in the speech bubbles.

> **We are your**
> s_____ (v18)

> **Don't b___**
> _____ (v19)

Joseph then told them that everything that happened had been part of **God's Plan**. (*More about that tomorrow.*)

Wow! The brothers had been worried that Joseph would want to pay them back. Instead, he forgave them and promised to look after their families.

What about you? Has anyone done or said something to hurt you? Do you feel like you want to pay them back?

THINK + PRAY

Ask God to help you to forgive them, and to show them you love them.

If you find this hard, talk to an older Christian about it.

DAY 64 MASTERPLAN

Find all of these people in the wordsearch.

Jacob
Joseph
Reuben
Judah
Simeon
Benjamin
Potiphar
Pharaoh

Some of these people had <u>wicked</u> plans—like Joseph's brothers and Potiphar's wife. But God used them all as part of **His good plan.**

READ
Genesis 50v20

This verse sums up the story of Joseph. Everything was part of God's masterplan.

Copy the leftover letters from the wordsearch.

G _ _ _   _ _   _ _ _ _

God is **King** of our world. He is in charge. His good plans always work out.

 Genesis 50v20

Think again about Joseph's words:

You meant evil against me, but God meant it for good.

THINK SPOT

These words were true for Joseph. And they are true for **Jesus** too. Jesus' enemies had a wicked plan to kill Jesus. They only meant it for evil. But **God** meant it for **good**. It was always God's good plan to send Jesus to die for us, so that we can be forgiven.

PRAY

Thank God for His great rescue plan. Thank Him for sending Jesus to die for you, so that you can be forgiven.

Use the Flag and Shape Codes to find two words.

— — — — —   — — — — — — —

Joseph **trusted** God to keep a very important **promise**:

READ
Genesis 50v22-26

What promise did Joseph believe that God would keep? (v24)

What did Joseph ask his brothers to do? (v25)

Carry my **b**_____ back to the land God promised.

Did you know?

This promise was kept 400 years later. When the Israelites left Egypt, they took Joseph's body with them. (*You can read about it in Exodus 13v19 and Joshua 24v32.*)

THINK SPOT

Genesis tells us about things that happened a very long time ago. (Joseph lived nearly 4000 years ago.) **But God doesn't change.** He stays the same. We have seen that God *always keeps His promises*, and that *His good plans always work out*. That was true 4000 years ago—and it's true today!

PRAY Thank God that He doesn't change, and that the things you have learned about Him in Genesis are still true today.

Want to know more?
For a free booklet about the **Big Picture** of the Bible write to us at XTB, The Good Book Company, Blenheim House, 1 Blenheim Road, Epsom, Surrey, KT19 9AP, UK   Or email us at: alison@thegoodbook.co.uk

TIME FOR MORE?

Have you read all 65 days of XTB?
Well done if you have!

How often do you use XTB?
- Every day?
- Nearly every day?
- Two or three times a week?
- Now and then?

XTB comes out every three months. If you've been using it every day, or nearly every day, that's great! You may still have a few weeks to wait before you get the next issue of XTB. But don't worry!—that's what the extra readings are for...

XTB TIME

When do you read XTB?

In the morning.

When I get back from school.

At bedtime.

EXTRA READINGS
The next four pages contain some extra Bible readings from the book of Psalms. If you read one each day, they will take you 26 days. Or you may want to read two or three each day. Or just pick a few to try. Whichever suits you best. There's a cracking wordsearch to solve too...

The extra readings start on the next page

THE LONGEST SONG...

On Days 18 to 20 we dipped into Psalm 19. In these 26 extra readings we're going to look at another Psalm.

How can it take 26 days to read just <u>one</u> Psalm?

Because Psalm 119 is the l-o-n-g-e-s-t Psalm in the Bible. It has 176 verses!

The ideas in the box will help you as you read Psalm 119...

PRAY Ask God to help you to understand what you read.

READ Read the Bible verses, and fill in the missing word in the puzzle.

THINK Think about what you have just read. Try to work out one main thing the writer is saying.

PRAY Thank God for what you have learned about Him.

There are 26 Bible readings on the next three pages. Part of each reading has been printed for you—but with a word missing. Fill in the missing words as you read the verses. Then see if you can find them all in the wordsearch below. Some are written backwards—or diagonally!

If you get stuck, check the answers at the end of Reading 26.

C	O	M	M	A	N	D	S	G	O	L	D	T	A	F
O	B	E	Y	M	U	M	D	R	O	W	S	E	A	A
M	E	C	O	M	P	A	S	S	I	O	N	V	N	I
M	G	B	E	V	O	L	H	M	A	N	D	E	E	T
A	S	I	S	T	H	E	G	O	O	D	V	R	W	H
N	R	B	I	O	E	L	A	W	Y	E	N	O	H	F
D	A	L	M	P	D	N	A	T	S	R	E	D	N	U
M	E	E	O	D	F	A	I	T	H	F	U	L	U	L
E	T	E	R	N	A	L	C	A	T	U	D	E	R	N
N	H	O	P	E	L	A	M	P	O	L	O	R	D	E
T	R	A	E	H	A	R	I	G	H	T	E	O	U	S
S	G	N	I	K	P	W	O	R	T	H	L	E	S	S

Tick the box when you have read the verses.

1 ☐ **Read Psalm 119v1-3**

The way to be happy is to live the way God tells us to live in His Law.

"Happy are those whose lives are faultless, who live according to the law of the L _ _ _ ." (v1)

2 ☐ **Read Psalm 119v4-8**

The writer of the psalm knew he couldn't follow God's ways without HUGE help from God.

"How I hope that I shall be f _ _ _ _ _ _ _ in keeping your instructions!" (v5)

3 ☐ **Read Psalm 119v9-16**

The psalm writer loved God's words so much, he learned them off by heart.

"I keep your law in my h _ _ _ _ so that I will not sin against you." (v11)

4 ☐ **Read Psalm 119v17-24**

The psalm writer longs to know and understand God's words to him.

"Open my eyes, so that I may see the W _ _ _ _ _ _ _ _ truths in your law." (v18)

5 ☐ **Read Psalm 119v25-32**

The writer of the psalm asks for help to understand God's words.

"Help me to U _ _ _ _ _ _ _ _ _ your laws, and I will meditate on your wonderful deeds." (v27)

6 ☐ **Read Psalm 119v33-40**

We need God's help to turn towards Him, and away from worthless things.

"Keep me from paying attention to what is W _ _ _ _ _ _ _ _ _ ." (v37)

7 ☐ **Read Psalm 119v41-48**

The writer of Psalm 119 trusts God's words. He will obey them, and tell others about them too.

"I will announce your commands to k _ _ _ _ and I will not be ashamed." (v46)

8 ☐ **Read Psalm 119v49-56**

The psalm writer knows that God's words bring life—even when he is suffering.

"Even in my suffering I was comforted because your p _ _ _ _ _ _ gave me life." (v50)

9 ☐ **Read Psalm 119v57-64**

God is a God of love...

"LORD, the earth is full of your constant l _ _ _ ; teach me your commandments." (v64)

10 ☐ **Read Psalm 119v65-68**

God is good, and everything God does is good.

"You are g _ _ _ and what you do is g _ _ _ ." (v68)

(*Note: This is the same word twice!*)

11 ☐ **Read Psalm 119v69-72**

God's words are far more precious than silver and gold!

"The l _ _ that you gave means more to me than all the money in the world." (v72)

12 ☐ **Read Psalm 119v73-80**

God always judges rightly. His laws are right and fair.

"I know that your judgements are r _ _ _ _ _ _ _ _ LORD." (v75)

13 ☐ **Read Psalm 119v81-88**

The psalm writer longs for God to rescue him. He has put his trust in God's word.

"My soul longs for your salvation; I place my trust in your w _ _ _ ." (v81)

14 ☐ **Read Psalm 119v89**

God's word has <u>always</u> been true and will be for <u>ever</u>!

"Your word, O LORD, will last for ever; it is e _ _ _ _ _ _ _ in heaven." (v89)

15 ☐ **Read Psalm 119v90-96**

God is always faithful. We can trust Him completely.

"Your f _ _ _ _ _ _ _ _ _ _ _ _ endures through all the ages; you have set the earth in place and it remains." (v90)

16 ☐ **Read Psalm 119v97-101**

The way to be wise is to obey God's words.

"I have greater wisdom than old men, because I o _ _ _ your commands." (v100)

17 ☐ **Read Psalm 119v102-104**

God's words are even better than your favourite food!

"How sweet is the taste of your instructions—sweeter even than h _ _ _ _ !" (v103)

18 ☐ **Read Psalm 119v105-112**

Just like a torch shows us the way to go, the Bible shows us the right way to live.

"Your word is a l _ _ _ to guide me and a light for my path." (v105)

19 ☐ **Read Psalm 119v113-120**

The psalm writer knows God has promised to rescue him. He has put his trust in God's promise.

"You are my defender and protector; I put my **h** _ _ _ in your promise." (v114)

20 ☐ **Read Psalm 119v121-128**

God's commands are more precious than pure gold.

"I love your commands more than **g** _ _ _ , more than the finest gold." (v127)

21 ☐ **Read Psalm 119v129-136**

Seeing how people disobey God's laws makes the writer cry with sorrow.

"My **t** _ _ _ _ _ pour down like a river, because people do not obey your law." (v136)

22 ☐ **Read Psalm 119v137-144**

Even when faced with great trouble, the psalm writer still delights in God's words.

"I am filled with trouble and anxiety, but your **C** _____ bring me joy." (v143)

23 ☐ **Read Psalm 119v145-152**

God's words last forever. They are always true and never fail.

"Long ago I learned about your instructions; you made them to last for **e** _ _ _ ." (v152)

24 ☐ **Read Psalm 119v153-160**

God is full of compassion. He is always kind and loving.

"But your **C** _ _ _ _ _ _ _ _ _ _ LORD is great." (v156)

25 ☐ **Read Psalm 119v161-168**

The psalm writer loves God's rules so much—he thanks God for them seven times a day! (Do you?)

"**S** _ _ _ _ times each day I thank you for your righteous judgements." (v164)

26 ☐ **Read Psalm 119v169-176**

The writer of Psalm 119 says he is like a lost sheep, who needs to be rescued. (You can read Jesus' story about the lost sheep in Luke 15v1-7.)

"I wander about like a lost **S** _ _ _ _ so come and look for me, your servant." (v176)

WHAT NEXT?

XTB comes out every three months. Each issue contains 65 full XTB pages, plus 26 days of extra readings. By the time you've used them all, the next issue of XTB will be available.

ISSUE THREE: *Comings and Goings*

Issue Three of XTB carries on in the books of Matthew and Acts. It also begins to explore the book of Exodus.

- Investigate more of Jesus' miracles and teaching in **Matthew's** Gospel.
- Escape from Egypt with the thrilling book of **Exodus**.
- Join Paul on a dangerous journey as you read more of the book of **Acts**.

Issue Three of XTB comes with a free *Bible Mini Map Book*.

Available from:
UK: www.thegoodbook.co.uk
North America: www.thegoodbook.com
Australia: www.thegoodbook.com.au
New Zealand: www.thegoodbook.co.nz

Look out for these special seasonal editions of XTB!

Christmas Unpacked

Three weeks of Bible readings to help you focus on what Christmas is really all about. Meet Dr. Luke as he tells you all about God's Rescue Plan. Find out WHO the Rescuer is and WHY we need rescuing. Comes *with free Rescue stickers.*

Easter Unscrambled

Unscramble the meaning of Easter with the help of Dr. Luke. Discover what the last part of Luke's book tells us about Who Jesus is and Why He came. Comes *with free Rescue stickers.*

Summer Signposts

A three week Summer Expedition to discover the real Jesus. Zoom in on the seven signposts from John's book about Jesus. Follow the clues to discover Who Jesus is and Why He came. Comes *with a free magnifying glass.*

Do you know any good jokes?
—send them in and they might appear in XTB!

Do you have any questions?
...about anything you've read in XTB.
—send them in and we'll do our best to answer them.

Write to: XTB, The Good Book Company, Blenheim House, 1 Blenheim Road, Epsom, Surrey, KT19 9AP, UK **or e-mail me:** alison@thegoodbook.co.uk